EMPLOYING PEOPLE WITH ASPERGER SYNDROME: A PRACTICAL GUIDE

prospects

The National
Autistic Society

Acknowledgements

Prospects and The National Autistic Society are grateful for all the patient hard work of Gill Spence, Justin Penney, Katie Wood and Catherine Burkin in the preparation of this book, and for all the contributions by Prospects' service users and their employers.

Designed by Column Communications

Illustrations by Steve Lockett

Printed by Crowes Complete Print

© The National Autistic Society 2005, Reprinted 2007

ISBN: 1 899280 72 3

Contents

Chapter 5: Successful management 45

Chapter 6: Support and further information 61

Index 69

Foreword

The first time that I heard of Asperger syndrome was from my friend Tim Olsen, whose family has had experience of Asperger syndrome. Tim asked if we would be prepared to take someone on for work experience who had the condition and so we worked together with Prospects to provide such placements. The experience of co-ordinating these placements has been a learning curve for me and has made me realise what a very valuable contribution people with Asperger syndrome can make in the workplace.

In Goldman Sachs, the motivation to employ people with Asperger syndrome came from an awareness that we do not operate in a vacuum. The make-up of our workforce should reflect the community we serve: we believe that the communication difficulties people with Asperger syndrome have should not be a barrier to them finding employment. Ours is a diversified organisation and this should be reflected in our work ethics.

Although some people with Asperger syndrome will require support in the workplace, my experience is that the main thing they need is the opportunity to prove their worth. Time and again the candidates Prospects has supplied have shown their ability to perform successfully at work and a number of people taken on for short placements have had their time with us extended.

I hope this book will encourage other employers to give people with Asperger syndrome a chance to prove their value. It is a decision I am convinced they will not regret.

Richard Bremer
Goldman Sachs International

Chapter 1: Introduction

Chapter summary

Purpose of this book

Asperger syndrome and employment

Moving towards diversity

Disability and the law

Who is covered by the law?

Discrimination and reasonable adjustments

Enforcement

New developments

Prospects

Purpose of this book

This book is designed to give employers, HR personnel and managers the tools they need to support individuals with Asperger syndrome from recruitment through to establishment in their jobs. It will also be useful to those employers who find a member of their workforce has recently been diagnosed with the condition. Everything written here is based on the years of experience gained by consultants at Prospects, The National Autistic Society's Employment Consultancy. Prospects' consultants support individuals with Asperger syndrome on a regular basis in a wide range of employment and education settings.

There are thought to be more than 250,000 people with Asperger syndrome in the UK. But specialist employment consultants, such as those at Prospects, can only support a small minority of them in finding work and settling into the workplace. This book aims to bridge the gap where such consultants are unavailable and provide guidance for all those involved in the recruitment and management of individuals with Asperger syndrome.

People with Asperger syndrome have many valuable skills and qualities that make them desirable employees. However, for some employers the recruitment of individuals with a disability will also be motivated by the wish to diversify their workforce or to fulfil their legal obligations under the *Disability Discrimination Act 1995*. Whatever the motive, by following the guidance in this book employers can get the best out of their employees with Asperger syndrome and ensure their decision to recruit them is one they do not regret.

The book can be read as a whole or dipped into for guidance on specific issues. It is a practical resource full of examples of how managers and colleagues have developed fruitful relationships with workers with Asperger syndrome.

Asperger syndrome and employment

Of the 250,000 people in the UK that have Asperger syndrome only 12% have full-time jobs, according to research carried out by The National Autistic Society in 2001. This is much lower than the 49% of people with general disabilities who are in employment.

Many people with Asperger syndrome have difficulty finding and retaining a job. The problem is not that they lack the skills or motivation to work, but that there is a lack of information, advice and practical support available that addresses their specific needs. Once employers are aware of these needs, there are a number of simple adjustments they can make. For the person with Asperger syndrome these adjustments may make the difference between success and failure in the workplace.

Despite their difficulties, increasing numbers of people with Asperger syndrome are working successfully. Prospects has provided training and support for many candidates, giving them the confidence to enter the world of work. However, there are many more candidates with Asperger syndrome who would like employment but have not yet been given a chance. With the UK's skills shortage looking set to worsen as the population ages, employers can no longer afford to ignore this undiscovered workforce. Indeed, many people with Asperger syndrome have skills that are in demand, for example in the field of information technology.

Moving towards diversity

There is growing evidence that employing people with a wide range of backgrounds and experience can make organisations more creative and improve their profitability. There is also increasing awareness among firms that, in order to respond to customer requirements, their staff should be as diverse as their customer base. These two incentives are leading many companies to adopt policies designed to boost their employment and promotion of people with disabilities, women and people from ethnic minorities. The government is leading this approach by setting targets to increase diversity across the civil service.

A further spur to diversity is the concept of corporate social responsibility (CSR). Most corporations espouse the ideal of CSR, which includes encouraging diversity alongside other social and environmental initiatives. Championing CSR has become an important aspect of corporate branding used to promote firms both to the public and to new staff who are attracted to employers who display ethical integrity. Adopting a diversity policy is therefore now recognised as an important step to attracting all new staff. When it comes to diversity, CSR is not simply about companies being do-gooders, it gives the opportunity for employers to find a new and valuable source of labour.

Many people with Asperger syndrome have skills that are keenly sought after in the workplace and making adjustments necessary for them to carry out their job can be easy. Employers who have taken up the challenge have reported improvements in communication generally throughout their organisations and in defining objectives – benefits that have arisen from the need for clear communication when employing individuals with Asperger syndrome.

Disability and the law

Who is covered by the law?

The *Disability Discrimination Act 1995* (DDA) is the current law that protects the interests of disabled people in employment. The rights and interests of people with Asperger syndrome are covered by this legislation.

The DDA gives disabled people protection from discrimination in:
- the way they are selected (including deliberate refusal to consider an application)
- the terms offered by the employer
- the way in which they receive job promotion, training, transfer or any other benefits.

The following chapters will show adjustments employers can make in these three areas to ensure they are fulfilling their obligations under the DDA in relation to people with Asperger syndrome.

The Act applies equally to employees who become disabled when established in a job. In the case of Asperger syndrome, which is a life-long condition, growing awareness of the condition means someone could be diagnosed after working for an organisation for many years. Once the condition is diagnosed employers are required to consider a number of 'reasonable adjustments' which could include:
- modifying the way a job is structured
- changing particular duties within a role
- providing retraining or redeployment to another post.

The Code of Practice on the employment of disabled people (which can be used in evidence in employment tribunal cases) indicates that employers should spend as much on retaining a member of staff who becomes disabled as they would on recruiting a replacement.

Discrimination and reasonable adjustments

In order not to discriminate against disabled people, employers:
- must not treat a disabled person less favourably because of a reason relating to his or her disability, without a justifiable reason
- must make reasonable adjustments to working conditions or the workplace where that would help to accommodate a particular disabled person
- must not victimise disabled workers because of their disability.

A 'reasonable adjustment' is a reasonable step to reduce or remove any substantial disadvantage caused to a disabled worker or job applicant by any of the employment arrangements.

Enforcement

Liability for committing an unlawful act of discrimination rests with the employer unless it can demonstrate to an employment tribunal that practicable steps were taken to prevent unlawful discrimination, for example if the employer had a clearly communicated equal opportunities policy which covered disability. If the employer can show such steps were taken, an employee responsible for an act of discrimination could be individually liable to pay compensation. There is no upper ceiling on compensation in discrimination cases. It is therefore vital for employers to ensure that managers receive disability awareness training.

New developments

From October 2004 the DDA applies to all employers, regardless of how many people they employ, except for the armed forces. It also covers practical work experience – whether paid or unpaid – and organisations that provide employment services, such as employment agencies and careers guidance services.

From the same date, all organisations that provide a service to the public will be required to make their services accessible to disabled people. The Government is keen to emphasise that this requirement is not just about physical access, such as installing a ramp for wheelchairs. It is about thinking 'outside the box' when it comes to catering for people with a range of different disabilities, for example providing Braille menus for the blind. Being informed about 'hidden disabilities' such as Asperger syndrome is particularly important when planning adjustments.

A Code of Practice provides guidance for employers on how to comply with the new provisions. The Code can be used in evidence in legal proceedings under the Act. It can be accessed via the Disability Rights Commission website (www.drc.org.uk).

A *Disability Discrimination Bill* is currently going through Parliament which, once enacted, will replace the current legislation. The new Act will place a positive duty on public bodies to promote equality of opportunity for disabled people. It is expected to come into force in 2006.

Prospects

Prospects is a specialised employment consultancy for people who have Asperger syndrome. It is part of The National Autistic Society (NAS), and was established in 1994. It currently has four branches in London, Glasgow, Sheffield and Manchester.

Prospects consultants provide work preparation training, assistance with job finding, and ongoing workplace support to adults with Asperger syndrome. They ensure that jobs are appropriate to the individual's skills and experience. Prospects can also provide training and consultancy services to managers and their teams.

Prospects has placed its clients with Asperger syndrome in a range of jobs in both the private and the public sectors. Many employers have benefited from its service including a leading investment bank, a major supermarket and the civil service.

Ten years of experience has made Prospects the leading UK expert on Asperger syndrome in the workplace. In recent years Prospects has experienced a growing demand for information about Asperger syndrome from employers. This book is its response to that demand and also stems from a wish to share best practice in employing people with Asperger syndrome.

Further information on Prospects' services is given in Chapter 6 on page 62.

Chapter 2: What is Asperger syndrome?

Chapter summary

Asperger syndrome

Social issues and communication

    Communicating by email

    Taking things literally

    Unwritten rules

A different way of thinking

    Understanding another's thoughts and feelings

    The importance of detail

    Obsessions and rituals

Stimuli and the work environment

Improving self-confidence

Asperger syndrome

Asperger syndrome is an autistic spectrum disorder (ASD) sometimes known as 'high-functioning autism'. An ASD is a life-long developmental disability that affects the way a person communicates and relates to people around them.

Asperger syndrome affects the individual's ability to understand and interpret the non-verbal behaviour, motivations and expectations of others. As a result social interaction may be confusing. Despite this, people with the condition are generally sociable and outgoing and often seek contact and friendship with other people.

Men are more likely than women to have Asperger syndrome, with some sources suggesting the ratio of men to women is as high as ten to one.

Some people with an ASD have an accompanying learning disability. By contrast people with Asperger syndrome tend to be of average or above average intelligence and often have skills that are valuable in the workplace.

People with an ASD often find it difficult to:
• communicate
• understand social relationships
• think in abstract and empathetic ways.

While people with Asperger syndrome share these impairments, they may manifest themselves in different ways and to different degrees. Some people will find communication, social relationships and abstract and empathetic thinking much easier than others. It is important for employers to consider each individual's particular needs so that appropriate adjustments can be made.

Although first described by Hans Asperger in 1944, it is only in recent years that Asperger syndrome has been widely recognised as a life-long condition. As a result many people are still undiagnosed and new diagnoses are being made all the time. Often people with Asperger syndrome were given incorrect diagnoses before the condition became widely recognised.

The most useful tool in tackling problems that may arise when employing someone with Asperger syndrome is awareness of the condition. It is often a hidden disability. People with Asperger syndrome frequently lack the confidence to ask for what they need, or lack an awareness of what their needs are. It is vital, therefore, that employers are aware of the issues and anticipate them. With sufficient and appropriate support people with Asperger syndrome have every chance of success in the workplace.

Social issues and communication

Many people with Asperger syndrome want to be sociable and enjoy human contact. However, they often find it hard to understand non-verbal signals, including facial expressions. They may also communicate or express themselves in an unconventional way. This makes it more difficult for them to form and maintain social relationships with people who are unaware of the hurdles they face. Social skills are something people with Asperger syndrome have to learn, just as another person might learn a new language.

People with Asperger syndrome can have difficulty knowing when and how to adapt their voice level to the situation. They may talk loudly or quietly all the time and they may talk in monotone. They might not take much notice of the reactions of people listening to them, talking persistently regardless of the listener's interest. This behaviour may seem insensitive but it is not deliberate.

Some people with Asperger syndrome do not like to be touched, while others do not understand physical boundaries and may 'invade another's space' or hug another person inappropriately.

Everyone will benefit if the person with Asperger syndrome is told in a friendly and straightforward way how to adapt his or her communication style.

Case study: Is it compulsory to talk?

When Peter started work at a local council office he didn't see any reason to talk to his colleagues. Social conversation was not part of his job description and seemed irrelevant to him.

His manager explained to him that when he was at work he was part of a team. His work performed a function within the organisation and could not be done without communicating with his colleagues.

He now understands this and does try to make small talk with his colleagues. He also understands the importance of communicating with his colleagues to keep them informed about his work and to get feedback.

Communicating by email

Written communication is often easier than spoken communication for people with Asperger syndrome because it does not involve interpreting body language or nuances of speech. Writing also gives the person the opportunity to compose his or her thoughts. Many people with Asperger syndrome enjoy using computers and so email can be an ideal form of communication.

Case study: Emails only please

Simon's job as an administrative officer involved him communicating with internal customers, but he did not feel confident about taking telephone calls.

Using the telephone requires immediate responses and instant processing that can be difficult for people with Asperger syndrome.

Simon's boss agreed that he could communicate using email instead. This simple adaptation gave him time to prepare what he wanted to say and to express his thoughts clearly.

Taking things literally

Often people with Asperger syndrome will take what people say literally. Common turns of phrase and metaphors such as 'she bit my head off' may be confusing or alarming to them. It is therefore best to avoid ornate or figurative language when speaking to them.

"Shortly after he started with us, Paul had a case of beetroot in his hands and asked me what I wanted done with it. I said flippantly 'just chuck it over there', which is what he did, literally throwing the case because that's what I'd asked him to do. What you really need to do is think two steps ahead when you're speaking to Paul." Gordon Sutters, Replenishment Manager, Sainsbury's

Case study: Warning hazardous bins!

After watching a health and safety video Lewis was convinced that the bins in his office were a hazard to his team's safety. The video warned that any objects left on the floor would obstruct movement around the office and could potentially cause someone to trip and injure themselves.

Looking around the office Lewis saw hazardous waste paper bins beside every desk. As a preventive measure he decided to tidy them all away. When Lewis's colleagues came into work after lunch they found their bins stacked neatly in the corner of the room.

Because of his Asperger syndrome Lewis had taken the video's recommendations literally. His behaviour was logical and sensible, but did not take account of the convention for the use of bins within the office layout.

Lewis's line manager took time to explain to him that the bins were necessary, and as long as they were not in positions where others were likely to trip over them they should be returned to their original places!

Unwritten rules

All jobs have unwritten 'rules', some of these are social and some are work-related. For instance, team members may make cups of tea and coffee for each other if they are having one themselves and someone would not normally enter another person's office without knocking first.

People with Asperger syndrome may not instinctively understand these social 'rules' and may need them to be explained. They also often do not recognise social hierarchies and therefore will address the cleaner and the chief executive in exactly the same manner. They may consider their job to be restricted to what is written in their job description or daily plan and not recognise the significance of social behaviour.

However, many people with Asperger syndrome will be aware that their difficulty in reading social cues can cause misunderstandings and will ask for reassurance that their behaviour is acceptable. Explaining the unwritten rules of the workplace can help to avoid any misunderstanding and encourage people with Asperger syndrome to fit in with their colleagues.

Case study: Right on time

Melissa was very accurate with her time-keeping. She arrived at work at precisely 9am every morning and left at 5pm every afternoon.

When a staff training course ended at 4pm, Melissa assumed she should go back to the office and work her full seven hours, even though she knew she wouldn't be back until shortly before 5pm.

Melissa did not understand the unwritten rule that if you are on a full day's training course you do not normally return to the office, even if the course finishes early.

So, while her colleagues headed for home, Melissa went back to work. She sat dutifully at her desk for a few minutes, busying herself until the clock struck 5pm.

The following day her colleagues who had also attended the course got a ribbing from the other workers in the office. "Where were you last night? Bunked off early did you?" they asked.

A different way of thinking

Psychologists define the third 'impairment' of Asperger syndrome as 'lack of imagination'.

The word 'impairment' is in quotation marks because not everyone with Asperger syndrome considers the differences in their thinking as an impairment. Some people with the condition think that the way their minds work is simply different, not worse than the way 'normal' people think. People with Asperger syndrome sometimes describe people whose minds work 'normally' as 'neurotypicals'. One person with the condition has even set up a website to encourage 'neurodiversity'.

The phrase 'lack of imagination' is also shown here in quotation marks because this definition is too narrow and misleading for many people with Asperger syndrome. It is too narrow because the 'impairment' covers a range of characteristics including difficulty with:

- abstract thinking
- taking on new ideas
- understanding other people's thoughts and feelings

- projecting themselves into the future
- using initiative.

The words 'lack of imagination' are misleading because, contrary to the psychologists' definition, many people with Asperger syndrome have active imaginations. They may also, however, have a tendency to develop narrow obsessional interests.

Understanding other people's thoughts and feelings

People with Asperger syndrome have difficulty understanding other people's thoughts, viewpoints, beliefs and emotions. They may therefore find it hard to empathise with others. This lack of understanding may make the person appear to be arrogant, self-centred or indifferent, but it is just a characteristic of the condition.

It is helpful to read what people with Asperger syndrome themselves say about the difficulty they experience in understanding others:

"The subtleties of emotion and facial expression are very hard for us to understand – if someone is smiling broadly, it is clear, but less obvious emotions are more difficult."

"We have trouble working out what other people know. We have more difficulty guessing what other people are thinking."

"The area of difficulty many of us have is in imagining the feelings of others."

The importance of detail

Detail is often vitally important to people with Asperger syndrome. They will follow exact processes accurately and adhere closely to what they have been taught. They will normally perform a procedure in the same way and to the same standard repeatedly.

Attention to detail is a positive attribute to bring to many tasks in the workplace. There may be whole areas of job knowledge in which workers with Asperger syndrome become experts, knowing more than either their colleagues or their bosses. The challenge for some people with Asperger syndrome will be to maintain their level of detail whilst completing tasks within a given time frame.

Case study: How many pens exactly?

Rajinder completes all tasks with extreme accuracy. In her job as administrative assistant she was asked to complete a stationery audit. She was given an Excel spreadsheet with separate cells for blue, red and black pens. She emailed each department asking for details of all the items in their stationery cupboards.

Some of the answers that came back were vague, not saying exactly how many pens were in stock, let alone what colour they were. The lack of detailed information made this task stressful for Rajinder. Because of her Asperger syndrome, she was unable to provide approximations. She also found it hard to understand why her colleagues were not more interested in giving her detailed information.

Rajinder talked through the task with her boss who gave her more information about the level of detail required. He said she only need record how many boxes of pens each department had, not the exact number of pens. He also told her how long it would be appropriate to spend on the task so that she could prioritise her work. With this extra briefing, Rajinder was able to complete the task successfully.

Obsessions and rituals

Many people with Asperger syndrome have obsessions and/or rituals that are part of their everyday life. This may create difficulties if the obsession or ritual affects their work, or upsets or irritates their colleagues. If this happens then a strategy will need to be devised to address the problem.

Example
A person with Asperger syndrome who had a tendency to pace up and down the office was helped to incorporate this into, 'pretending to go and pick something up from the printer' or 'walking to the toilets and back'.

To read a case study about a strategy used to address an issue raised by an obsessional interest turn to page 52, Chapter 5, Case study: Dog racing talk restricted.

Stimuli and the work environment

People with Asperger syndrome often have a heightened sensitivity to sounds, tastes, smells and sights. Sensory stimuli that most people can usually filter out may become overpowering for a person with this condition and affect their ability to concentrate.

Some do not like sitting with their back to the rest of the room because they are anxious about people coming up behind them. It is therefore worth checking with workers who have the condition whether they are able to concentrate and work comfortably in their immediate environment. Where necessary, consider making an adaptation or moving them to another part of the office.

Case study: The flashing telephone

Guy worked in a large, open plan office with many telephones ringing around him. He found it hard to distinguish the ring tone of his telephone from all the others. All the phones sounded the same to him. Guy's boss put a flashing light on his phone so he would be sure to know when it was ringing.

A simpler adjustment to help a person distinguish his or her telephone from the rest would be to change the ringtone. Many telephones allow the user to do this.

People who have heightened sensory perception may also find the volume of telephone ringing too high. This problem can easily be addressed by turning down the volume on their phones and those of their immediate colleagues.

Simple adjustments like these can make it much easier for someone with Asperger syndrome to concentrate.

Improving self-confidence

Many people with Asperger syndrome have been out of work for a long time or have never had a job. Often they have suffered bullying at school, college and work due to their condition, especially when it was not diagnosed in childhood. With no explanation for their different behaviour, they are simply regarded as odd or awkward and picked on by their peers and colleagues. As a result of these negative experiences low confidence is often an issue.

Building confidence is an important part of helping people with Asperger syndrome to succeed in the workplace. As with any worker, confidence can be built by giving the person achievable tasks and consistent, positive feedback about their work and their value as a member of the team.

Good quality training on Asperger syndrome will promote understanding and help ensure the worker with Asperger syndrome is protected from harassment by colleagues. The training should make clear that bullying and intimidation will not be tolerated in the workplace.

Case study: Cultivating confidence

As a child Steve was moved from foster home to foster home as few people understood him or could deal with the difficulties associated with his Asperger syndrome, then an unrecognised condition. He was never at school long enough to gain any formal qualifications and came to Prospects with just a few basic skills certificates. However, despite his limited CV, Steve was determined to find work.

Steve's lack of self-confidence made it difficult for him to sell himself at interview. Prospects worked to improve his confidence and found him a temporary contract as a production line worker. The firm he worked for was extremely helpful and worked with Prospects so that his time at the factory was as successful as possible.

After just a few days at work Steve's confidence started to rise. He was doing a brilliant job and making friends. The manufacturing firm gave Steve positive feedback and were impressed with his enthusiasm and effort.

After only three weeks Steve was awarded 'Employee of the week'. This exceptional award gave Steve a real boost as it gave him the much-needed reassurance that he was able to succeed.

The contract came to an end but the experience of being successfully employed and being awarded 'Employee of the week' has given Steve the confidence he needs when applying for jobs in the future.

Chapter 3: Recruitment and selection

Chapter summary

The right person for the job

    Skills and abilities

    Types of suitable employment

Adapting recruitment procedures

    Job advertisements

    Application forms

    Interviews

    Tests and work trials

The issue of disclosure

Can the job be adapted?

The right person for the job

Clearly the point of the recruitment process is to find the person with the best skills and abilities to do the job. People with Asperger syndrome have many abilities, skills and other qualities to offer but it is vital to find a job in which they will flourish and use their abilities to the best advantage.

Skills and abilities

People with Asperger syndrome are generally highly conscientious, trustworthy and honest. They are also usually of average or above average intelligence. Often they develop an enthusiasm for a particular subject and learn it very thoroughly.

There is a rare condition known as savant syndrome that occasionally occurs in people with an autistic disorder. This condition came to the public's attention in the popular US film *Rain Man*. Dustin Hoffman portrayed Raymond Babbit, an autistic savant, who had a phenomenal memory for baseball statistics and the phone book. Babbit could also count cards as they were rapidly shuffled in a Las Vegas casino. While such abilities are rare among people with Asperger syndrome, they do often have excellent memories, especially for facts.

Those people with Asperger syndrome who have very strong interests will probably be happiest and most productive doing work that harnesses those interests. They may find it hard to see the relevance of other subjects and activities. However, many people with the condition will happily carry out a variety of tasks. A preference for routine may mean that many gladly perform duties that seem repetitive and boring to others.

"Mark joined Max Fordham's in March 2002 as a drawing filer, quickly grasping the complex procedure. He applies care and attention to detail, constantly using his initiative to improve efficiency. He regularly attends progress meetings where his input is invaluable and he supervises temporary cover within his group." Margaret Jones, Partner/Head of Administration, Max Fordham LLP

Case study: Just ask Jim

Civil service boss David was apprehensive about taking on Jim because he wasn't sure how his Asperger syndrome would affect his performance at work. But Jim soon revealed star qualities both in his memory for detail and the accuracy of his work.

Jim was a payment and receipts clerk and soon the whole department came to rely on his encyclopaedic knowledge of forms.

David checked Jim's work carefully at first, but he gradually realised it simply wasn't necessary – it was always 100% accurate. Jim surprised his colleagues in another way because, in his case, Asperger syndrome did not impair his social skills or his ability to understand sarcasm, so they had some good laughs.

People with Asperger syndrome often offer some of the following skills and abilities:
- reliability
- motivation to work
- a high level of technical ability
- accuracy and attention to detail
- good concentration on 'routines' or 'procedures'
- a memory for facts and figures
- a logical approach to tasks
- manual dexterity.

"I have always been impressed with Reggie's enthusiasm, zeal and product knowledge – particularly the latter, which is much better than mine!" Nick Johnston, Receiving Department, Tower Records

Employing someone with Asperger syndrome can also help employers think about and improve communication within the workplace, as it is necessary for communication with people with Asperger syndrome to be very clear.

Types of suitable employment

Depending on the individual, any job could be considered for a person with Asperger syndrome. In general it has been found they are more suited to jobs where there is an element of routine and where there is a right or wrong way of doing things. Jobs that involve fast decision-making, multi-tasking and strong interpersonal skills are less likely to suit them.

People with Asperger syndrome excel in jobs that draw on their strengths. They often have strong analytical skills and a logical approach to problem-solving. They may offer skills in accounting, bookkeeping, engineering, statistics and research. People with the condition can do well as computer programmers and software designers. There are also those who are very creative and work as graphic designers, musicians and artists. Clearly the right job for the individual will depend on his or her level of skill, education and interests.

Types of task that are likely to be suitable for people with Asperger syndrome include:

- tasks for which attention to detail and accuracy is required, eg data input, word processing and research
- routine and repetitive tasks, eg filing, photocopying, scanning, sorting and sending out information
- tasks involving numbers/statistics/facts, eg finance/accounting
- tasks where there is a clear procedure to follow, eg dealing with incoming/ outgoing post, archiving/library work
- highly structured tasks where there is a right and wrong way of doing something, eg IT support/programming.

Prospects has placed the majority of its clients in administrative and clerical posts. It has also placed many clients in stock control and warehouse jobs. The employment consultancy has been surprised to find that, despite their difficulties with communication, a number of people with Asperger syndrome have done well in customer-facing roles, for example customer reception assistant and shop assistant. Other posts individual clients have taken on include writer, postman, proof reader, seamstress, librarian and statistician.

Main areas in which Prospects has found work for people with Asperger syndrome:

- clerical and administrative roles
- data entry
- IT support
- jobs involving statistics
- cheque clearance
- computer programming
- warehouse work
- customer service.

Case study: On the right track

Customer Reception Assistant at Paddington Station was not an obvious choice of job for someone with Asperger syndrome. The position involved dealing with customer queries and sometimes with angry customers. However, with careful training on how to handle different types of query and ongoing feedback and support, David has been able to perform the role to a consistently high standard.

David knows the train times by heart and can therefore answer customers' queries immediately. Despite this, incredulous customers often ask him to look things up 'just to be sure'.

When it comes to angry customers, David's Asperger syndrome is actually an advantage. He has a detachment from other people's emotions which means he is not upset by customers' anger and is therefore able to handle difficulties in a calm and sensible way.

David is a valued member of the Paddington Station team.

Adapting recruitment procedures

Despite having a great deal to offer employers, people with Asperger syndrome often find getting a job much harder than doing or keeping one. As a result employers miss out on a potential pool of talent. It can be relatively easy to adjust the recruitment process to ensure that people with Asperger syndrome can apply for jobs, and that their work potential is not overlooked.

Job advertisements

Job advertisements often contain confusing jargon, or stipulate unnecessary qualifications or exceptional communication skills. Whilst excellent communication skills are needed for roles involving negotiation or presentations, for many more routine jobs they will not be necessary. For example 'excellent interpersonal and communication skills' and 'excellent team-working skills' are probably not essential for a filing clerk, but it is not unusual to find these requirements in a job description. Employers are urged to establish which skills are essential for the role and to present these in a clearly worded advertisement.

Some employers have objected to changing interview questions on the ground that it would be unfair to other candidates and therefore a breach of their equal opportunities policy. In fact, adjusting interview questions so that they can be readily understood and answered by a candidate with Asperger syndrome is a 'reasonable adjustment' under the *Disability Discrimination Act 1995*, and is a good example of providing equal opportunities for candidates.

The interview may also be an opportunity to find out what types of adjustments are needed to enable the candidate with Asperger syndrome to succeed in the job. However, in many cases, candidates will not know what adjustments are needed, being as yet unfamiliar with all the requirements of the job and the working environment. Whilst adjustments for sensory and physical disabilities are generally straightforward, for example Braille for the blind and ramps for wheelchairs, adjustments for people with Asperger syndrome will be more varied and will depend on the needs of the individual. By listening to those needs, and responding creatively to any problems, adjustments can be made as and when the need arises.

Case study: Interview and test combined

Chloe knew she had the qualifications and the experience for the position of records clerk, but she was concerned about the interview. She had good administrative skills and had been complimented on her performance in her work placement, but she found it difficult to express her strengths to employers.

The organisation advertising the records clerk vacancy agreed to adapt their standard interview so that Chloe could do a practical work-based task combined with a modified interview.

In the interview, rather than asking open questions, the interviewers asked Chloe specific questions relating to her past work experience. That way Chloe was able to explain what she had achieved in her previous job.

In her practical test Chloe demonstrated the necessary skills for the job. She even performed the work more quickly than some existing employees!

Chloe was offered the job of records clerk on the day of her interview and test.

Supporters

Many people with Asperger syndrome perform much better at interview if they have a supporter with them who can rephrase questions and help them to understand exactly what the interviewer wants. The supporter might be a friend, a family member or an employment consultant.

A supporter is not there to answer for the person with Asperger syndrome, but simply to rephrase the question or help the person to communicate with the interview panel. Many employers have found supporters invaluable in understanding what people with Asperger syndrome have to offer. Allowing a person to have a supporter with them is also likely to be a 'reasonable adjustment' under the terms of the *Disability Discrimination Act 1995*.

The Government's 'Access to Work' programme offers communicator support at interview (CSI) which meets the full cost of hiring an interpreter for a disabled person to remove barriers to communication at interview. For more information see Chapter 6.

Tests and work trials

Tests will often give candidates with Asperger syndrome a better opportunity to display their ability than interviews alone. For example, work sample tests and in-tray tests are often used in conjunction with interviews for administrative posts.

People with Asperger syndrome may benefit from being given extra time for written tests. Sometimes it takes longer for them to develop a train of thought and they may also need extra time to switch thought processes. An extra 25% of time could be allowed – 50% may be too much. It is best to ask people whether they need extra time as they may not. The person setting the test could say: "We can offer extra time because we understand that some people with Asperger syndrome need it."

Test questions in which people are asked to give an answer on a scale of one to ten or multiple choice questions should be avoided as they involve a type of thinking that is difficult for people with Asperger syndrome. A short question and answer format is more suitable.

Another way of establishing whether a candidate with Asperger syndrome is suitable for the job is to give them a trial period. This could be a day, a week or a month. Prospects has found that many of its clients who have undergone work trials have been offered the job at the end of the trial period.

Case study: Putting workplace skills to the test

Dele did not come across well in his interview. He tended to either answer questions inappropriately or answer 'yes' and 'no' without elaborating about his experience.

However, his prospective employers were extremely impressed when Dele scored 100% in the filing test as this was significantly higher than the scores of other candidates.

The firm had been made aware of the fact that it would be difficult to assess Dele's ability using an interview alone and had offered Dele a work trial as an alternative method of assessing his suitability for the job. Dele's managers were delighted with the accuracy and reliability he displayed during his trial period.

Dele still works for the the same company today as a filing clerk, performing with consistent accuracy and good humour in a useful job that many people might find tedious.

Psychometric tests

Psychometric tests are now a standard part of the recruitment process for many jobs. In our increasingly service-led economy, the emphasis is often not on practical skills but on 'soft' skills – invisible characteristics such as 'vision', 'persuasiveness' or 'leadership'. In order to establish whether the candidate has these qualities employers often use psychometric testing.

While practical tests can give people with Asperger syndrome the chance to demonstrate their skills, psychometric tests are unlikely to be useful and could even be confusing because the questions are abstract and there is no right or wrong answer. The world of psychometric profiling is unlikely to be one to which people with Asperger syndrome can relate and, because social skills are an area of difficulty for them, it would be unfair to assess them on this basis.

The issue of disclosure

An employer has the right to ask whether a candidate has a disability as long as everybody is asked the same question. However, a candidate can choose not to disclose this information. Application forms should give candidates the opportunity to disclose if they so wish. Prospects always advises people with Asperger syndrome to disclose their condition in order to give employers the chance to support them. Candidates may refer to their condition as Asperger syndrome, autism, high-functioning autism or ASD.

If people with Asperger syndrome choose not to tell employers about their condition they will clearly not get any additional support. They may decide to disclose at a later date or an employer may learn that an existing employee has been diagnosed with the condition. As soon as the condition is brought to the employer's attention, the employer is required to consider making any necessary adjustments to accommodate the person's needs.

Can the job be adapted?

Allocating some of a disabled person's duties to another person could be considered to be a reasonable adjustment under the *Disability Discrimination Act 1995*. In the case of a person with Asperger syndrome, the types of duty that might be reallocated might be those involving social skills or strategic planning; the decision would depend on the individual's abilities and limitations. It would also depend on the willingness and ability of someone else within the organisation to take on the extra duties or to exchange duties. It is important for the employer to adopt a flexible approach wherever possible and not to require the candidate to match the job description perfectly.

Case study: A duty shared

Yousef was delighted to get a job as an administrative assistant at a local solicitor's but, because of his Asperger syndrome, he had difficulty coping with telephone queries.

Yousef's employer asked the three assistants who worked with him whether they would be willing to take his calls in exchange for Yousef doing some of their filing.

The other assistants were happy to swap the work as they found filing boring. In this way an adjustment was made that suited everyone.

Notes

Chapter 4: Getting started

Chapter summary

Areas where support may be needed

Finding the right level of support

   Job coaching and mentoring

Planning the first day

Creating a working file

Induction

Training strategies

Checklists for getting started

Areas where support may be needed

The *Disability Discrimination Act 1995* gives a list of examples of adjustments which employers may need to make to support individuals with disabilities. Reasonable adjustments for someone with Asperger syndrome are usually simple to make and seldom costly. The following list shows types of adjustment that may be particularly useful for workers with Asperger syndrome:

- allocating some of the disabled person's duties to another person
- allowing the person to be absent during working hours for rehabilitation, assessment or treatment
- giving or arranging for the person to be given training
- modifying instructions or reference manuals (eg by providing written as well as verbal instructions)
- modifying procedures for testing assessment
- providing supervision (eg a job coach or support worker)
- altering the person's working hours (eg adjusting working hours if a person finds it stressful to travel in the rush hour)
- transferring the person to fill an existing vacancy
- assigning the person to a different place of work (eg if the person has difficulty making long journeys by public transport).

Finding the right level of support

Workers with Asperger syndrome will need different levels of support depending on the severity of their condition and the extent to which it impacts on their working lives. Some may need no support at all, many will be able to work independently after an initial period of close support, while for others some form of ongoing help will be necessary.

Support may be either internal, in the form of a manager or a buddy who works alongside the person, or it may be external, in the form of a specialist consultant or job coach.

Managers may need to assess the support requirements of their workers with Asperger syndrome by observing and talking to them over the course of a few days. The manager should consider the worker's need for support both in gaining work skills, such as time management, and in gaining social skills. Workers are unlikely to know exactly what support they need and the process of finding the right level of support should be based on consultation between worker and manager. Where their Asperger syndrome is quite mild they may simply need some extra help from the manager. For instance they may benefit from instructions being given in writing. In other cases external support can provide invaluable help, particularly during the first few weeks at work.

Employers can apply for support from the Government's 'Access to Work' programme, which aims to 'meet the additional employment costs resulting from disability'.

Getting the level of support right is vital to the success of a job placement. If an individual with Asperger syndrome does not have the support he or she needs, it could not only lead to failure in the job but could also damage that person's confidence and future prospects. It would also be costly for the employer who has gone to the expense of hiring and training the person.

"When I was first told I was going to be Victoria's manager I thought I would have to invest a lot of time and energy in training and explaining everything to her. I found the reality was that I didn't. It was no more than anybody else coming into the Inland Revenue completely new. The only difference was that sometimes I had to write things down for her." Dianne Mitchell, Trainer, The Inland Revenue

Job coaching and mentoring

Coaching and mentoring are increasingly popular forms of training for all staff. While coaching helps staff develop job-specific skills, mentoring is often used to help familiarise new recruits with an organisation. These forms of one-to-one training can be particularly useful to workers with Asperger syndrome.

"Coaching is the fastest growing training practice." Chartered Institute of Personnel Development

A specialist consultant or job coach can play a vital role in helping a worker with Asperger syndrome settle into a new job. Where the worker was recruited via a specialist employment consultancy, the employment consultant may act as a coach, perhaps visiting the worker on a daily basis for the first few days of a placement and on a regular basis thereafter depending on their needs. Consultants will discuss with workers how they are settling in and any difficulties they have encountered. The consultant will also normally be available by telephone should the worker need this support. The consultant may support the employer as well as the employee, for example by educating line managers and colleagues about the condition, and helping them deal with any problems that arise.

When meeting a worker with Asperger syndrome and a job coach together, managers should remember that the coach is providing a service to the worker. It would be inappropriate to address questions of the 'does she take sugar' kind to the coach. The worker with Asperger syndrome should be addressed and the coach will assist only where necessary.

Before phasing out their support, job coaches will ensure workers can handle the job independently and have a support network within the organisation. It is often useful for the worker and the employer to be able to telephone or email the job coach with certain problems, even after the worker has settled into the job.

The Government's 'Access to Work' programme offers a support worker to provide specialist coaching for people with disabilities and will pay up to 100% of the approved costs entailed in providing support for a new worker. Details of the programme can be found in Chapter 6.

"I think having a support worker with Victoria was very helpful, someone independent to refer to who could help not just Victoria, but us as well." Dianne Mitchell, Trainer, The Inland Revenue

Buddies
One of the most common forms of mentoring is to appoint a 'buddy' as a point of reference for a new worker. A buddy is a person the new recruit can go to when he or she has questions and who will help that person adapt to the new environment. A buddy can play an important role for a person with Asperger syndrome who is likely to have difficulty adjusting to the work environment and fitting in to the social scene.

Where a job coach is employed the buddy may take over from that person as the main point of reference for the worker. Because people with Asperger syndrome may have difficulty developing relationships, it is important they have somebody they know they can go to for advice and support.

The buddy should be chosen carefully and fully briefed about the nature of the individual's condition. Buddies will find the experience a valuable means of developing their own skills, particularly management and support skills. It will also help them understand how disability can affect a person in the workplace.

"These are individuals who can make a difference but have never been given the chance and like you and me they welcome the support to get them started out in life." Richard Bremer, Knowledge Manager, Goldman Sachs International

Planning the first day

Managers may be surprised by how quickly and enthusiastically their new recruit with Asperger syndrome gets down to work. Often managers 'take it easy' on a new worker during the first few days, giving them time to settle in and familiarise themselves with new systems, but people with Asperger syndrome may well not be aware that this is the manager's intention. Usually they will be very work focused and will want to get on with a task straight away, concentrating on it until it is completed and then asking what they should do next. They may well find unstructured time difficult to deal with. It is therefore helpful that the manager has plenty of tasks or one substantial task prepared for them to work on.

It is also important that the manager knows exactly how these tasks should be carried out. Giving the worker a rough outline and assuming he or she will know what is intended is a recipe for failure. The first step is for the manager to be clear exactly what needs to be done. It is helpful to break down each task and provide a written checklist or procedural outline for the employee to follow. For more details on communicating with people with Asperger syndrome see Chapter 5.

"We went through the job description word for word so David knew what he was expected to do, what he felt he could do and what he might have problems with."
Michael Daymond, Store Manager, John Jones artSauce

Creating a working file

Supplying a file in which new workers can make training notes and keep checklists and guidelines is good working practice. As with so many other strategies in this book, what is a useful aid for many workers is a vital tool for the worker with Asperger syndrome.

The working file is likely to be referred to frequently by workers with Asperger syndrome who may find verbal communication difficult but will be eager to do things correctly. Often their tactic for ensuring they are doing their job properly is to ask

"After my first day, I was convinced that I was going to fail. Like many people who have been out of work for a long time or have never had meaningful employment, I worried that I was unemployable or unable. As I began my training at the job, I felt overwhelmed because of the amount of information I had to try and take in. Early on in the job (day two), I telephoned Judith [employment consultant] from a public phone and told her I was not coping. But I had not understood the fact that everyone takes time, maybe months, to learn a new job. I had simply failed to realise the fact that nobody would get fired because they were not perfect after the first two days. Thankfully, I did not give up and I am now enjoying my job very much." Ben Good, Messenger

Training strategies

People with Asperger syndrome often benefit from one-to-one training. Certain types of group training activity may be difficult for them. Their presence in a group training session could, in some cases, also be problematic for the trainer. This is because some people with Asperger syndrome have a tendency to ask a lot of questions. This may not necessarily mean they do not understand what is being taught, they may simply be seeking reassurance that they have fully grasped the issue. Other people with the condition may struggle to learn in a group situation but not tell anyone about their difficulty. Having said this, there are other people with the condition who will thrive in a group training session and contribute constructively to discussions. It is vital to treat each person as an individual.

The best approach, where possible, is for the employer to allow the individual to choose the form of training or instruction he or she receives. Workers could be asked whether they prefer written or verbal instruction, and whether they want notes provided or can write their own. Often people with Asperger syndrome will not ask for any special help themselves, so it is important to make clear the choices available, eg 'would you prefer one-to-one training, e-learning or to participate in group training'. If there are aspects of training that can be done by e-learning this may well suit the worker with Asperger syndrome, eg induction training about policies and procedures might be given via the organisation's intranet.

Training tips:
- break a task down into easy-to-follow steps
- ensure training exercises are concrete not abstract – hypothetical problems may cause difficulties
- ensure training is practical and specific.

CHECKLISTS FOR GETTING STARTED

The new recruit with Asperger syndrome is likely to need special help in the following areas:

- *orientation* – finding out where things/people are

- *job analysis* – guidelines/breakdowns for each task within the job

- *structure* – breakdown and organisation of the day (time table/plan etc)

- *social training/awareness* – understanding the unwritten rules of the workplace, teamwork dynamics and how to seek help in appropriate ways (see Chapter 5).

Disability awareness training could be provided to colleagues where the worker wishes them to know about his or her condition. The training should be specific to the strengths, needs and limitations of the individual.

The employer can help the new recruit with Asperger syndrome by:

- providing a 'buddy' to act as a mentor during the first weeks

- giving the worker clear directions with additional instructions, such as written steps or checklists

- offering honest and constructive feedback about things that are going well and areas of work or social behaviour that need to change

- being patient and supportive

- including the new worker in the organisation's social events

- liaising with the employment consultant or job coach (if the worker has such support)

- identifying the training that is needed and making the necessary provision.

Strategies for success

Support or absence of support from a line manager can make or break a job for a worker with Asperger syndrome. A supportive manager who communicates clearly will ensure that person becomes and remains a valuable member of the team.

Working with someone with Asperger syndrome is also likely to benefit the manager. Managers who have gained an understanding of the communication difficulties people with Asperger syndrome experience say they have learnt to communicate with their whole team more effectively.

The strategies outlined in this chapter have been used by many line managers to support people with Asperger syndrome in their jobs. However, it must be remembered that each person is an individual and strategies that work for one person may not work for another.

Tips for successful communication

The following tips will help managers who need to convey instructions to workers with Asperger syndrome, ensuring they get their message across and get the best out of the individual. It is worth considering these points before any meeting or discussion.

Do not make assumptions

We tend to assume other people know certain things. Some of these things might be described as 'common sense'. For example most people will check there is paper in the machine before starting to photocopy. It is safer not to assume that workers with Asperger syndrome have this 'common sense'. It is important for managers to convey each step in a process and ensure they are not making any assumptions about what the person knows. If in doubt, it is best to ask.

Example
An office junior at a solicitor's office was asked to wash the cups after a meeting. The sink had a pile of dishes in it. Because of his Asperger syndrome, the office junior took the direction literally and only washed the cups. Much to his boss's dismay he left the rest of the dishes in the sink.

Be direct

In order to be polite most of us have learnt to ask for things in an indirect way, so instead of saying, "I want you to send me a document," we say, "I would be grateful if you could send me a document." The conditional wording shows that we are not assuming our correspondent will automatically do our bidding. However, this type of indirect speech is not helpful to workers with Asperger syndrome. They understand much better if given direct instructions.

Example
It is better to say, "I want you to stay until you have finished that project," rather than "It would be good if that project could be done today." If the latter form of speech is used workers with Asperger syndrome may not take any action because they may not realise they are being asked to do something.

Be precise

When giving instructions or explanations it is best to be precise and specific and say *exactly* what is required.

Example
It is better to say, "Can you photocopy this three times and give the copies to Mary, Sam and Ahmed" rather than, "Make sure everybody has a copy of this."

Avoid figurative speech

People with Asperger syndrome usually take what other people say literally. So if a manager says, "I could have killed her," the individual with Asperger syndrome may be alarmed because he or she does not realise the manager is speaking metaphorically. If the manager says, "I'll be back in a minute," that person may look at his or her watch and expect the manager to return in exactly one minute. The worker will not necessarily understand that in common parlance a minute is used as a general term for a short period of time.

Case study: Don't miss the bus!

People with Asperger syndrome often become obsessively enthusiastic about one subject and for Douglas it was buses. He loved them so much that he took five different buses on his way to work despite the fact the most direct route only involved two. Although he left two hours to get to the office, the bus connections were often poor and Douglas kept on arriving late for work.

Doreen, Douglas's supervisor, realised what was happening but thought it was something she had to accept because of his Asperger syndrome, so she did not talk to him about it.

Although Doreen's intentions were good, she was actually not doing Douglas any favours, since he was not learning the importance of good time-keeping in the workplace.

After talking to Prospects, Doreen resolved the problem by making it clear to Douglas, in a firm but friendly way, that he needed to be at work on time. Douglas was encouraged to travel to work using the most direct bus route and to pursue his personal interest in buses on his homeward journey instead.

Douglas responded well to his talk with Doreen and now he normally arrives at work on time.

"We have to adjust the way we think and not make assumptions about what people understand. Once things have been made clear and the boundaries are set things usually work really well." Justin Penney, Employment Consultant, Prospects

Explaining the quality expected

Workers with Asperger syndrome are often highly meticulous and may become very anxious if they are unable to perform perfectly. For example, a worker who starts work at 9am may become much more stressed than a colleague if he or she is late due to a delayed train or bus. If a worker is concerned about his or her performance, it may be helpful to explain that perfection is not always possible in every task every time. For example, where the worker is late, the manager could explain that it is acceptable to be late occasionally if the person makes up the time by staying later or coming in earlier the following day.

> # CHECKLIST FOR SETTING TASKS
>
> When setting a task the manager should:
> - explain the purpose of the task
> - explain each step of the process
> - state the expected outcome or end product
> - convey the quality expected
> - set a time-frame for completion
> - check the instructions have been understood.

Appropriate topics of conversation

Sometimes workers with Asperger syndrome may say or ask things that colleagues judge to be inappropriate, too personal, odd or even bizarre. It is important to be aware that this is not done on purpose to annoy or upset other people but is merely based on a lack of understanding about accepted 'rules of conversation'.

It may be useful to provide the worker with a list of inappropriate topics of conversation for the workplace, alongside a list of appropriate topics.

Example
Inappropriate topics of conversation:
- *age* – asking people how old they are
- *money* – asking people how much they earn, or how much their house or car cost
- *appearance* – commenting on another person's appearance
- *personal life* – asking about people's marriages or relationships
- *personal hygiene issues.*

Appropriate topics of conversation:
- asking people if they had a good weekend or holiday
- music, films, theatre, books, TV programmes
- shared interests and hobbies
- asking others about their role in the organisation, what they do, how long they have worked there etc
- the weather.

Prioritising

Some people with Asperger syndrome may have difficulty in prioritising tasks. Managers can help by explaining which jobs need to be done first. For example, a worker with Asperger syndrome who was employed as a park keeper was given a map of the park showing the high and low priority areas for maintenance. Areas the public used most frequently were indicated as high priority, while other areas were low priority. The worker was also given lists of tasks that should be given priority during each season of the year.

Managing breaks and lunchtimes

Often workers with Asperger syndrome find breaks and lunchtimes more difficult to manage than the actual work tasks they are employed to do. This is because these times are usually unstructured social times, when colleagues chat, laugh and relax over coffee or lunch. Workers with Asperger syndrome often lack the skills required for this type of social interaction and are unsure of what is expected of them.

Providing some guidelines, such as key 'opening phrases' for conversation may help them gain confidence to take part (see 'Appropriate topics of conversation' on page 51). If people prefer to do their own thing during these times, the manager could suggest alternative activities such as crosswords, reading a magazine, listening to a personal stereo or going for a short walk.

Time off work

Workers with Asperger syndrome may need to be reminded to take their full annual leave as many of them will see little point in leisure time or holidays. Their conscientiousness also means that, despite their disability, people with Asperger syndrome generally have an excellent attendance record.

"Zoe has hardly any time off sick. If Zoe's off work, we know that she's really ill. Her attitude to work is really responsible. She has shown clear commitment to Evans."
Valerie Topping, Stockroom Supervisor, Evans

Change management

People with Asperger syndrome are likely to find change more difficult to cope with than people who do not have the condition. Changes ranging from a colleague leaving to moving offices or the threat of redundancy could cause them a great deal of anxiety. In large organisations rumours of changes that may or may not be true often spread and workers with Asperger syndrome may take such rumours very seriously. It is therefore important to inform them in advance of any changes and dispel any unfounded anxieties.

When informing workers of changes, they should be given an explanation of why the changes are necessary and prior warning of the timetable for the changes taking place. If there are further developments, workers should be kept updated of these. This is important, not only because workers may become anxious when changes occur that they are unprepared for, but also because their communication difficulties mean they may misunderstand what they have been told by colleagues or have overheard.

Feedback and appraisal

Line managers and colleagues need to be prepared to give feedback which is honest, constructive and consistent. Workers with Asperger syndrome will not be proficient at picking up social cues and may assume their performance is acceptable unless explicitly told otherwise. In other cases, workers with low self-esteem may be anxious about whether they are living up to expectations, in which case positive feedback is vital.

If a person behaves inappropriately or completes a task incorrectly, it is essential that he or she is told tactfully but clearly what is wrong, and what should be done instead. The matter should be addressed at the time or as soon as possible afterwards. This can be a difficult area to tackle, but when done well will be a support, helping people with Asperger syndrome to develop both their work and their social skills. Similarly, if somebody has done something well, it is helpful to give positive feedback.

"Having positive feedback really helps, a simple 'you're doing great' is fine. Not just letting people know when things are going wrong, but to actually give positive feedback as well. Also, it helps if I am kept informed directly about exactly what is happening." Alex Cockell, Application Support Analyst

- Give clear feedback – for example if you feel your colleague has taken too much time checking a piece of work when this was not necessary, then be honest and tell the person.
- Remember to give positive feedback when things have been done well, since this may not always be obvious to someone with Asperger syndrome.
- Be aware that Asperger syndrome may prevent your colleague from being able to understand team dynamics, or the 'unwritten' rules of the workplace. For example, your colleague may have to work a bit harder than others when making 'small talk' with colleagues during break/lunchtimes. Despite this, please remember that many people with Asperger syndrome want to be sociable and enjoy contact with others.

If problems arise

There may be occasions when, despite following these guidelines, problems arise either in relation to job tasks or relationships with colleagues. Most of these problems can be dealt with swiftly and tactfully. For example, if a worker with Asperger syndrome seems aloof or disinterested in talking to colleagues, or says the wrong thing, colleagues can be reminded that this is unlikely to be intentional, but is simply a manifestation of the difficulties that person has with communication.

Similarly, a worker may try too hard to fit in and irritate colleagues by seeming to 'muscle in' on a conversation. Such situations can often be defused by patience, understanding and a clear explanation of boundaries. Other staff may also need to be made aware that their reactions to the worker may have a strong impact on that person's behaviour and performance.

If a worker with Asperger syndrome becomes anxious, or there is an increase in rituals such as pacing around the office, try to find out what is causing the problem. One-to-one sessions are probably best for this. The manager may need to think laterally. For example, the stress may not be caused by a difficulty in the job, but by a colleague not being explicit in instructions, by things not working (such as IT breakdowns), or by difficulties in getting to work. Try to think 'outside the box', but avoid being intrusive and prying into the person's life or work unnecessarily.

Case study: Five steps to successful line management

Over the two years that Gerald has worked for the local council he has built up an excellent rapport with his line manager Peter.

We asked Peter to tell us the strategies that he found most successful when working with Gerald. He outlined five secrets to their success.

1   Regular meetings – these allow Peter to give Gerald regular positive feedback and discuss any aspects of his work that could be done differently. They help Gerald to monitor his performance at work and make changes where necessary.
2   Written instructions – Peter ensures that Gerald is given written instructions for any new tasks or changes to the way he is to carry out his work.
3   Involvement in the team – Peter ensures that Gerald is involved in team activities. He is aware that Gerald finds communicating in a group difficult and so thinks carefully about different ways of involving him.
4   One-to-one training – when Gerald needs training, Peter arranges for it to be given on a one-to-one basis so that Gerald receives individual attention and has time to process new information.
5   Staff awareness – when new staff join the team Peter with Gerald's agreement makes sure they are briefed about Gerald's Asperger syndrome in order to raise awareness and prevent any potential misunderstandings.

CHECKLIST FOR MANAGERS

To give workers with Asperger syndrome the best chance to perform well in their job:
- make the rules of behaviour explicit
- introduce new tasks in a structured way
- use written or graphical instructions
- provide checklists and a daily or weekly timetable
- prepare for and explain any changes in the workplace
- supervise closely at first
- give frequent and immediate feedback
- ensure you are consistent in your dealings with the person.

What support is available to employers?

Getting the right level of support is vital to the success of employing an individual with Asperger syndrome. The advice of a specialist employment consultant can help both worker and employer to overcome any problems that arise. Employers should also take advantage of the financial support the Government offers which will assuage any additional costs involved in providing training and support to the worker.

There are two main sources of support: specialist employment agencies and Government employment schemes. The employment agencies, which are generally themselves Government-funded, may be the main source of support for the employer. Alternatively, the employer may be introduced to a candidate or gain support from one of the Jobcentre Plus employment schemes for the disabled.

Specialist employment agencies

Across the UK there are various employment agencies that specialise in working with disabled people, including those with Asperger syndrome. The leading employment consultancy for people with Asperger syndrome is Prospects. Prospects has branches in London, Manchester, Glasgow and Sheffield. Where there is no Prospects branch close to the employer, or where Prospects is unable to meet the employer's need, there are other agencies that can offer support to employers of workers with a range of disabilities including Asperger syndrome.

Prospects

Prospects employment consultancy is run by The National Autistic Society. It works with people with Asperger syndrome, helping them to find and keep jobs, and offering support to their employers and colleagues. Prospects can help employers by providing professional advice, support and training to managers and their teams, and by offering training and on the job support to people with Asperger syndrome.

Prospects employs a team of specialist employment consultants who work with people with Asperger syndrome who have demonstrated the motivation and skills needed to secure and retain a job. It works intensively with candidates to get to know their skills and abilities and provides tailor-made training courses before matching the person to an appropriate job. Prospects has helped hundreds of people with Asperger syndrome to get jobs ranging from administration and IT to journalism.

Prospects helps employers maximise the skills of workers with Asperger syndrome by assessing the work environment, advising on any adaptations or adjustments, and advising on the recruitment process. It helps employers set up:

- work experience placements
- short-term contracts
- permanent contracts.

Prospects' employment consultants also provide:

- training in autistic spectrum disorders
- support and training for line managers and colleagues
- team briefings
- one-to-one support for the worker with Asperger syndrome in the workplace
- follow-up support and on-call services for line managers, colleagues and workers with Asperger syndrome
- career development.

The cost of a Prospects' employment consultant to support the worker in the workplace may be met by Government-funded schemes such as 'Access to Work'.

To contact Prospects see the 'Useful addresses' section on page 67.

Other non-specialist employment agencies

Mencap Pathway offers support to employers of people with disabilities in various parts of the UK. To find out the address of the nearest office in their area, employers can call: 01709 830 956.

Shaw Trust offers a range of services designed to help employers recruit, train and retain disabled and disadvantaged people. It can be contacted on 01225 716 350 or visit its website at: www.shaw-trust.org.uk

Remploy provides a network of employment consultants. Tel: 0845 845 2211; email: interwork.osc@remploy.co.uk; website: www.remploy.co.uk

Government support

Most job centres and Jobcentre Plus offices have a Disability Employment Adviser (DEA) who specialises in helping people with disabilities to get work and advises both disabled job seekers and employers. DEAs can provide information on any support that is available in the local area. They can also advise on Government schemes that offer practical and financial support to employers.

Access to Work grants can pay for up to 100% of extra employment costs. For a person with Asperger syndrome, these could include the costs of any specialist training or coaching, or for additional costs of the employee's travel to work.

DEAs can provide more information about Access to Work and how employers can apply for it.

New Deal for Disabled People
People who are in receipt of health-related benefits, either through a disability or health condition, can get into work with the help of New Deal. The programme is entirely voluntary.

Specialist job brokers from employment agencies can match disabled people to vacancies and support both employer and employee for the first six months. Advice is also available to employers on how to adapt the workplace to enable recruitment or retention of a person with a disability.

Please note that although we have provided information on the various Government schemes outlined above which is correct when going to press, The National Autistic Society and Prospects cannot make specific recommendations about them as different employers and individuals have their own needs, concerns and experiences. For up-to-date current schemes please also check the Jobcentre Plus website: www.jobcentreplus.gov.uk

Information about Asperger syndrome

The National Autistic Society website includes information about Asperger syndrome and support and services available in the UK: www.autism.org.uk

AS-IF is a website written and edited by a person with Asperger syndrome which may help 'neurotypicals' (people who do not have the condition) to understand what it is like: www.neurodiversitynow.net

Online Asperger Syndrome Information and Support (OASIS) is a US site that contains some useful information and definitions: www.udel.edu/bkirby/asperger/aswhatisit.html

Information about employing people with disabilities

The civil service has created a useful online 'toolkit' for employing people with disabilities at www.diversity-whatworks.gov.uk/toolkit/foreword.asp

For information on new legislation and its implications for employers visit: www.disability.gov.uk or the Disability Rights Commission website at: www.drc.org.uk

Employers can join the Employers' Forum on Disability to learn from the experience of other organisations and to keep up to date with disability issues. Visit the website at: www.employers-forum.co.uk

Useful addresses

Jobcentre Plus services
New Deal helpline: 0845 606 2626 (7am-11pm seven days a week)
Jobcentre Plus Employer Direct helpline: 0845 601 2001 (8am-8pm Monday to Friday).
Websites: www.jobcentreplus.gov.uk (information on WORKSTEP, the JIS and Access to Work can be found on this site), www.newdeal.gov.uk

The National Autistic Society
393 City Road
London EC1V 1NG
Tel: 020 7833 2299
Fax: 020 7833 9666
Email: nas@nas.org.uk
Website: www.autism.org.uk

Prospects London
Studio 8
The Ivories
6-8 Northampton Street
London N1 2HY
Tel: 020 7704 7450
Fax: 020 7359 9440
Email: Prospects-London@nas.org.uk
Website: www.autism.org.uk/prospects/london

Prospects Glasgow
1st Floor
Central Chambers
109 Hope Street
Glasgow G2 6LL
Tel: 0141 248 1725
Fax: 0141 221 8118
Email: Prospects-Glasgow@nas.org.uk
Website: www.autism.org.uk/prospects/glasgow

Prospects Step Into Work Project
Ground Floor
Coburg House
2 St Andrews Court
Leeds LS3 1JY
Tel: 0113 236 6767
Fax: 0113 236 6760
Email: Prospects-Leeds@nas.org.uk

Prospects Manchester
Anglo House
Chapel Road
Manchester M22 4JN
Tel: 0161 998 0577
Fax: 0161 945 3038
Email: Prospects-Manchester@nas.org.uk
Website: www.autism.org.uk/prospects/manchester

Prospects Sheffield
Sheffield Hallam University
School of Education
35 Broomgrove Road
Sheffield S10 2NA
Tel: 0114 225 5695
Fax: 0114 225 5696
Email: Prospects-Sheffield@nas.org.uk
Website: www.autism.org.uk/prospects/sheffield

Index